AF256901

Alone With My Thoughts

Poems By Eric Hannan

2019

To family and friends who've pushed me to do great
things and never let me settle for less than the best.

I'm a rich man to have so many people in my life who
encourage me and help me be better. There are too many
to name, but you know how you are. From the bottom of
my heart, thank you, thank you, thank you.

Peace.

Contents

"If courage is a value of yours, then you have no choice but to show up and be seen."

Brene Brown

Alone With My Thoughts

I sit alone with my thoughts,
With nothing clamoring for my attention.
Solitude,
Peace
Serenity, even.

I think of times gone by,
Decisions made
Choices avoided
The consequences of them all…

I stroll through the perfect paradise of my memories
From which I can never be expelled.
Alone with my thoughts I am free
Free to gaze upon His splendor,
Free to ponder His majesty,
Free to consider His Holiness
Free to be overwhelmed by it all.

Alone with my thoughts I am who I wish to be,
Undistracted by the failures that plague my reality.
Here I can dream of all that God has called me to,
The good works He's set before me to do.

Alone with my thoughts…
Though overwhelmed by the presence of the Spirit,
Here to empower
Here to give boldness
Here to break the power of sin.

Alone with my thoughts.
I can deal with things that matter most
My love for my family,
My church,
And yes, maybe even a spouse.

Alone with my thoughts is when I'm most true,
When I'm not hiding my innermost thoughts from all of you.
There's no wall to hide behind,
No people who can hurt,
It's just me and my thoughts

Alone with my thoughts I am free to dream
To dream of the way I wish things could be
To dream of what I hope may be
To dream of what I long for things to be.

It's good to be alone with my thoughts,
No TV vying for my attention,
No Facebook statuses competing for my consideration,
No songs on the radio to heighten my emotions.
It's good to be alone with my thoughts,
For here I am in complete control of what I think.

A Break from the Ordinary

It's a phenomenon,
A break from the ordinary
An interruption to the daily process of life

It's longed for all year long
yet only seemingly savored for a couple fleeting moments

For a brief moment
We have a glimpse
A portal into the possible
A glance at what could be...

The stress of work feels miles away
Arguments with family a distant memory
Bitterness and anger are replaced with joy and love

A shift of focus,
From yourself to the joy of others.
An intentional picking of gifts to elicit excitement and joy
The celebration of family
Of loved ones
Of memories

Stories shared around the table
Laughter filling the air
A sense of togetherness
Christmas.
A break from the ordinary
An interruption
But should it be?

A Star Sparkles

A star sparkles brightly in the night,
The beauty of the moment, a treasured sight.
The sun starts its ascent,
Ahhhhh,
The start of a brand new day.

The worries and cares of the day start to flow…
But hang on, don't forget the Way you know.

Down on your knees you fall,
Never before have you felt so tall.
As the time you spent on your knees before your Savior.
He wraps you up,
Holds you tight,
Gives you the energy and courage to fight.

The day wears on,
As you worship the Son,
Unknowingly touching lives of those around.
Soon, one day, you will see their star,
Shining brightly in the night,
Knowing God used you and helped you to put up the
fight.
The beauty of that moment,
What a treasured sight.

Bombarded

Stuck
Thoughts racing through my mind
I know what's right.

Stretching
Straining
Trying to break through the haze of thoughts.

I know what I need
but I'm trapped
Stuck
Bombarded with thoughts.

Pushing
Plodding
Treading my way through.

Deep breath,
Silence the thoughts
Slowly count to three
Step forward, make a choice
The one that is right for me.

Brother

A bond between two men
There is no stronger
It comes from living a life
shoulder to shoulder
come what may,
through thick and thin
a bond that will never be broken,
that's what it is, to call you Brother

Brother
A man I would die for
A man I would cry for
A man I would give all I have for
That's what it means, to call you Brother

Brother
I need you to know
I'm not as strong without you.
When you're with me,
I can stare death in the face
Without the slightest ounce of fear.

I feel like I can conquer any battle,
Because I know you'll always be near,
Standing with me,
Shoulder to shoulder,
For that is why I call you Brother.

Brother
I will stand with you during your darkest hour
I will fight for you when you're hurting
I will protect you when you're down
I will be there
To encourage you
To push you
To stand with you
And pick you up
To give you hope,
When all seems lost
I will be there,
Shoulder to shoulder
Because that's what it means, to call you Brother.

Captured

Though I briefly met you
Your smile is indelibly etched in my memory

Though I don't know much about you,
Thoughts about you flood my mind

Though we didn't talk for long,
The sound of your voice has stuck in my soul

Though it was a brief encounter,
The beauty of who you are has lasted for hours

Though you may never remember my name,
Your name is written on my heart

Thought it was a moment in time,
Time stands still when I think about that moment

Crying Out

Pretense and fear,
Doubts,
Anxiety
Clamor around in your ears.
It's been hidden for so long,
Days turned to weeks
To months
To years.
The longing and yearning,
To know
And be fully known.

      Deep cries out to deep

Stepping out from behind the wall,
Vulnerable.
Emotions stand on the brink of overload,
Doubts
Anxiety
Past hurts and disappointments flood your thoughts,
Overwhelming you with it all.
You take a step back to safety,
Almost behind the wall.

      Deep cries out to deep

Stop.
Listen closely…
Something captures your attention,

It's the unrelenting pull,
To know
And be fully known
The call of another soul.

     Deep cries out to deep

Cautious yet brave,
Slowly peeling back all the layers
Pensive, afraid
Yes somehow fulfilled
And assuaged.
The connecting of two souls
Brings the deepest parts alive

     Deep cries out to deep

To be fully known,
To balance trust and fear
To be so open
And give all you have,
Sharing all you hold so dear
Your soul stands naked,
Vulnerable

Deep cries out to deep

The connection of two souls,
An intricate melody,
Separated the parts are hollow,
Together they produce a gorgeous symphony.
Boldness together,
Each part complimenting the other,
Intertwined
Inseparable
The connection of two souls
Knowing
And being known.
A beautiful melody
A glorious song
Awakening the soul

Deep cries out to deep,
Vulnerable and refreshed,
Rejuvenated
Restored.

Exposed

Emotions stand on the brink of overload
Fears nearly grip your soul
Thoughts race through your mind at a blinding pace
Tears flood your eyes

Vulnerable
Not knowing which way to turn
Fears of the past swarm the present
The unknown future looms on the horizon
Like a dark rain cloud slowly moving in

There's a strange comfort in the night time,
The darkness offers a place to hide
The darkness doesn't penetrate,
It envelopes, it covers
But strangely doesn't soothe

But something's different now,
You can no longer hide
The darkness that once offered some solace
Only causes more unrest

The voice of your Father calls

The light exposes your heart,
Penetrates through the fears,
Cuts through the emotions,
Slows the thoughts,

Though the tears remain,
You are not alone
For there's One that knows your heart,
Feels your pain
He has wept
And cried
And knows what it's like to be utterly alone

"His yoke is easy
His burden is light
He offers rest for the weary,
Restoration for the broken,
Sight for the blind
Liberty for the captives,
And love, genuine love for the lonely."

Emotions informed by truth burst with joy
Fears replaced with Power for "perfect love casts out fear
Thoughts taken captive, set on Christ above"
Tears flood your eyes, for such a display of love

Fading Light

The light quickly faded over the hill,
But I never did get my fill.
I loved him so very much,
And he reached out,
My heart he did touch.
With a bright smile on his face,
He lit up every place.
He brought so much cheer,
No one could shed a tear.
He laughed, he cried,
And then he soon died.
But his memory lives strong,
From dusk till dawn.
His loving face,
His saving grace.
He was a gift from above,
A big bundle of love.
Now he is in heaven with thee,
Peaceful and happy as can be!

To Greg, a Gift of Love

Hope

The beauty of your eyes captures my gaze,
Your smile melts away the pain.
The sound of your voice assuages my fears,
The touch of your hand removes all tension,
Just knowing you're here
Brings a peace and calmness to my anxious soul.

Emotions stand on the brink of overload,
So much to say
But no words to express

How do you describe a love that burns from deep within?
A love that stirs the soul,
A love that longs to be poured out,
To protect, and guard,
To honor and cherish,
To give all I have for you…
What words can possible express?

Your gentle touch brings me back to you.

As I gaze into your eyes, I can see the questions,
The fears…
Why would you love me?
Will you always?
Can I trust you to protect me?
To honor and cherish me?
Why would you want to?

You are a treasure,
The pearl of greatest price.
I long to hold you,
To adore you,
To honor and protect you,
To quiet your fears,
To wipe away all your tears,
With a love like you've never known.

Mountain Top

A mountain top experience,
The height of God's glory on full display
The Gospel preached
The lost saved

Overwhelming…

God moved in mighty ways,
Your soul tasted of things unknown
Your spirit soared to worlds unknown,
Your heart forever marked with the memory of those precious
little ones

Your soul longs…

But then it's back to the old mundane,
A taste of heaven impressed on your soul,
A piece of your heart left with the precious little ones
The magnificence of God's glory seems to be waning though
As its back to the old mundane

Your spirit yearns…

For more of Him,
What used to be can't be any longer
Mediocrity just isn't good enough
Just getting by won't cut it
A taste of heaven fuels your passion
Jolted

By the force of the reality you live in
Surrounded by pain
Plagued by death
Heart broken by sin

Lift up your eyes…

My child, lift up your eyes
You aren't coming back to the old mundane
For my precious child, you will never be the same
The things you saw
The lives you touched
Have forever changed you and set a fire ablaze

Ignited with a passion…

For a kingdom that cannot be shaken
With a message that will change the world
Yes, even your world
A message of hope
A message of peace
A message of love like the lost has never known

Empowered…

By my spirit
With the same power that rose Christ
To change the mundane
And make it new

A New Song…

A New Song I put in your heart

A song of love,
Genuine love
Real love
Unfading love
A love that will touch the deepest parts
Of a lonely and depressed heart

The Mountain Top…

A taste of heaven
An energizer for the soul

A balm to the spirit
A fuel for the heart
A fanning into flame the gifts,
The gifts that I have placed in you

Ask Boldly…

To change the mundane
For My Glory to be on full display
For the Gospel to be preached
For the lost to be saved

Nothing to Give

Nothing to give,
But everything to offer
For only one thing in this world can satisfy.

Riches I have not,
Fame I care not about,
Possessions are meaningless.

"Silver and gold have I not,
But what I do have,
I give freely,
In the name of Jesus…"

I have nothing to give you,
But everything to offer you

The American Dream,
A life of luxury, leisure
I cannot promise
Nor do I pursue
"I count it all as loss
Compared to knowing You"

I have nothing to give to you,
But everything to offer
For the surpassing greatness
Of knowing Christ Jesus my Lord.
His loving kindness is better than life itself

I may never be famous,
I may never be rich,
I may never have the nicest house,
The nicest car
But what I do have exceeds it all by far.

I have nothing to give to you,
But everything to offer,
For I have found a great treasure,
The pearl of greatest price
"Silver and gold have I not,
But what I do have, I give to you freely"
His name is Jesus, to whom none can compare.

No Words

My heart beats with anticipation,
Yet the words won't come.
My palms sweat, and my knees knock,
Yet the words won't come.
I see you approaching,
Yet the words won't come.
I see your heart deep in your eyes.
The hurt, the pain, the longing, the desire,
Yet the words won't come.
So fragile, yet so strong,
Your beauty is forever marked on my soul.
The beauty of that moment,
No words could describe,
Maybe one day, it could be just you and I.

Piercing

The day wears on, distractions all around…
Bills need paid, dogs need fed, house needs cleaned…
Anxiety and stress start to crowd my mind,
Myriads of thoughts competing for my attention.

Then a still small voice I hear in my ear…
The sound of your voice pierces my soul…
The worries quickly fade away to distant memories….
Waves of peace engulf my being,
As words of Truth flow from your lips…
My heart bursts with joy
As the praises of our King are read.

Words though small, pierce my soul…
Causing my mind to wander…
Wouldn't it be nice…

All too soon the night comes to an end,
I lay awake, in hopes of capturing the sound of your voice….
But alas, I fall asleep, wishing it didn't have to end.

My heart yearns as the day wears on…
Anxieties and stress start to crowd my mind…
But soon, they fade as you once again
Pierce my soul with your still small voice.

Safe

I hear my heart beat,
The tick of the clock,
The rush of the breeze
And in the stillness

Í hear my Savior say
"I love you Child,
You are mine.
I chose you from the very beginning,
You are mine.
You and I are going to do great and mighty things,
You are mine."

As my heart beats,
And the clock ticks,
The breeze rushes,
My soul is still and quiet,
Resting in the arms of my Savior.

Secure

I long to gaze into your eyes
For they tell the story,
They speak of times gone by.
Stories of hurt and pain,
Love and gain,
All told with a knowing gaze.

Your eyes ask the questions,
Of what, when and how.
Your beauty radiates as the
Passion of your soul springs forth.

But your eyes, they tell of longings for something more.
So I bring you close, and hold you tight,
In my arms you'll be secure,
As I hold you,
Oh so gentle,
Yet so firm.
I never want to let you go,
For in my arms you'll be secure.

Set Apart

Chosen by God,
Crafted by his hands
Molded for a purpose
Called for a reason

Set apart by his plans,
He called you by name
To be a daughter of the King

Fully restored,
A new creation
Mourning turned to joy

A faint spirit turned to praise

What was old has gone
What is new has come
The past destroyed
Sins forgiven
A new day has begun

No guilt
No shame
No condemnation
A new day has arrived

Hope springs eternal

As each new day begins
His mercies are new

His faithfulness great
As his steadfast love is poured out on you.

Quieted by his love,
Your spirit now bursts with joy
Your smile is a balm to a hurting soul
Highlighting your genuine love

To look into your eyes now is to see the heart of God
To see a love that's genuine
And a compassion that's gentle
With mercy overflowing
All because of the work of the Son

The Healing Road

Broken and fragile,
Pieces tearfully put back together
Hope clung to with a broken heart
Yearning... Hoping...
Crying out for a brand new start

New Day, New mercies,
Hope springs eternal
As the old is left behind,
A new day has begun

Slowly stepping forward
Faith built in your heart
With every cautious step,
Hoping your foot finds solid ground again

Storm clouds fill the horizon behind you,
Clear skies are up ahead
Each small step brings healing,
The haze that once did cover you,
Begins to drift and is even slowly fading

The Voice of your Heavenly Father calls,
Penetrating to the deepest parts,
And calms your hurting soul.
He's leading you, and guiding you
As you walk along the path to healing.

But the healing road feels treacherous,
Not much different than before
The Hurt
The Pain,
The Tears and all the Sorrows,
Still cloud your mind and
Swarm your soul
As you look ahead and begin
To worry about tomorrow

Shh – Comes the command
Of your loving Heavenly Father.
He calls you,
He calls you by name,
Proclaiming you are his Child.
"He rejoices over you with loud singing,
He quiets you with his love."
The burdens you carry:
The Hurt, the Pain,
The tears and all the sorrows,
He takes from you,
And puts them on his Son,
For you to no longer carry.

The healing road brings promise,
A hope and a fresh desire,
To live again
And love once more….
As you rest at his feet,
In awe, In love
Causing you simply to admire

A brand new start has come,
As the Mercies wash over you again,
The hope that once seemed distant,
Now rests firmly in your soul.

The Hole I Know

The hole I know
is better than the world I don't.
I know the shadows, the surrounding,
the pain.

Everyday I struggle and strain,
to lift myself from this place,
and examine the new terrain

But as I climb out of the hole I know,
my strength is sapped
my energy gone,
my courage low.

I want to see things new,
but I have nothing left to give,
to see the things in view.
Disheveled and forlorn,
I climb back down
resigned to the hole I know.

Then one day…
The light seemed brighter,
dispelling the shrouds of comfort
of the hole I knew and
with every step and every pull,
my strength and courage grew.

The hole I knew was gone from sight
ahead of me the world anew.

The Rebel is a Wall

The Rebel stands alone, though surrounded by throngs of
people,
Seeming to stand confident and strong

That's what people see from the outside anyways.

With the wall comes comfort
For nothing unwanted can come in.
A sense of security rests behind the wall,
For behind the wall the Rebel is in complete control.
Peace reigns behind the wall,
For nothing comes close enough to cause unrest.

That's what people see from the outside anyways.

The wall, from afar, looks solid and immovable,
Impenetrable to the curious eye
To climb it is too high
To go around it is too wide
The wall seems insurmountable

That's what people see from the outside anyways.

The Rebel stands alone,
Yet longs for something more.
The wall they've built keeps the people out,
        Yet their heart craves to see what love is all about.
Letting the people in…
would mean to trust and risk being hurt yet again.

Questions cloud the Rebel's mind
Fear closes in
Without the wall, what might the people find?

They long for someone to see what is behind the wall.

The comfort of the wall no longer satisfies,
          A sense of peace and unrest begin to intensify.
As the Rebel stands alone, behind the wall they've built,
Their heart bursts for something more,
To be a part of something,
To be loved by someone
Or at least to be noticed by a few.

What will people see now that they are no longer behind the
wall?
The Rebel stands alone…

The Secret, Quiet Place

I long to be there,
In my secret, quiet place.
I long to be there,
Trapped by your embrace.
No worries, no cares,
I can look upon your face,
In my secret, quiet place.
I gaze upon your glory,
In my secret, quiet place.
The hurt, the pain, the sorrow slowly drift away.
As I meditate on your unfailing love,
In my secret, quiet place.
Your voice calms my soul,
Your words penetrate my heart,
Your goodness overwhelms my thoughts,
Your holiness radiates with purity.
Oh how I long to be there,
Long for your embrace,
Long to hear your voice,
Long to touch your face,
I long to cry with you,
Worship you…
One day I will be with you.
But for now,
I'll meet you there,
In my secret, quiet place.

The Sparrow

The storm rages outside,
Tearing apart all in its path,
Yet peace reigns inside.
The wind howls fiercely,
Yet peace reigns quietly.
The rain beats downward against the earth,
Yet peace reigns inside.
Though things crash in all round you,
Peace reigns inside.
Dreams are crushed, and hopes are dashed,
Yet peace reigns inside.
People look at you,
They wonder why, how, what for?
Peace reigns inside…
Why they ask?
"For His eye is on the Sparrow,
and I know He watches me!"

Thoughts

A penny for your thoughts….
What are your dreams,
your hopes, your desires…
What do you wish for,
hope for, long for?

Thoughts so precious, so dear,
I will always keep them near.

A quarter for your thoughts,
The price is higher,
And so are the desires.
I cling to every word,
As you share a part of your soul.
So fragile and so beautiful,
Are the thoughts and desires….
Maybe…one day..

A dollar for your thoughts?
The increased price brings more emotions,
More hopes, more desires.
I sit and listen, handling your heart with care.
No worries, no fears….

The price of a penny,
The worth of quarter,
The value of a dollar,
All fall short to describe the worth,
To be trusted with your thoughts,
your hopes, your dreams, your desires.

Time Stands Still

Time stands still when I look into your eyes,
Cares and concerns fade,
Pain is washed away.

To look into your eyes is to see the beauty of your soul,
To see the passion that fuels the fire,
Of your love
And your deepest desires.

Your eyes paint a picture,
They narrate a story,
Broken pieces line the way,
A fragile heart and a passionate love
That you long to give away.
Grit determination sees you through,
As you navigate this path alone.

I lose myself as I look into your eyes,
There's a sparkle
And a twinkle
That brightens up the skies.
Nothing else matters as I gaze into your eyes.

To look into your eyes makes time stand still...

Time

Tick… tock
Tick…tock
Seconds turn to minutes
Minutes to hours,
Hours to days,
Days to months,
Months to years,
Years to a lifetime.
And it's all gone too quick.
Our life is like a vapor,
Here today,
but gone tomorrow.

Time goes by,
Never to return again.
You can't stop it,
Buy it,
Return it,
Or redeem it.
You can only live it.
Yesterday will never return,
tomorrow will never be today.
All you have is right now.

Stuck in this endless cycle,
Wanting to get out.
Every day is the same:
Thinking about yesterday,

Looking forward to tomorrow,
Wondering what I should do today.

Tick… tock
Tick……tock
Tick………tock
Tick………….

The clock stops…

Eternity begins

Unexplainable

Unexplainable,
Yet words try to explain.
Overwhelming,
But fulfilling at the same time.
Painful,
But love that overflows.
Unseen,
Yet felt by all.
Innocent,
Yet slain like a criminal.
Pure,
But took on the sin of us all.
Mysterious,
Yet revealed in love.
Uncreated,
Yet created all.
Eternal,
But reveals himself to us in time.
Man,
Yet fully God.
Unexplainable,
But words are not enough...

Unknown

The moonlight glitters over the water top
Can you feel the coolness of the sand?
We stroll aimlessly over the dunes…
Wondering, thinking, wishing…
Shh…listen…
The waves crash carelessly on the shore,
The wind blows briskly through the air..
The sea rages with mystery, yet sits in calm…
I look into your eyes, they tell the story…
Slowly we sink down onto the sand,
Staring into the starry night…
I hold you close, wrap you tight,
In my arms you are secure…
I begin to stroke my fingers through your hair,
Wondering, thinking, wishing…
The softness of your hair reminds me of the
Beauty and gentleness of your soul…
How I wish I could hold you forever…
But the night will soon end, and we will part…
Leaving me Wondering, thinking, wishing…

Worthy is the Lamb

All nations cry out
All of the people shout,
With one voice,
the saints sing.
As they join in the chorus,
Praise sounds from east to west.
Shouts of worthy…
Glory…
Honor and Praise
fills the skies.
The deafening roar grows more intense,
As worship of the Holy God goes on.
From eternity past,
to eternity future,
His name is worthy to be praised.

The roar is silenced with a wave of awe,
As the sacrificial lamb stands beside the throne.
His wounds still showing,
But his body not broken
The wounds send out an eternal declaration:
It is finished!!
The battle is over!
The victory is ours!

To sing of such a sweet salvation,
And be with him there
Shouts of worthy once again fill the air,
Another deafening roar…
Worthy is the Lamb

Striving After the Wind

Ever chasing,
But never receiving
Always starting,
But never arriving
Turning the corner,
But never making it around the bend
Always hoping,
But never fulfilled
Always reaching,
But never grasping

It's like striving after the wind.

The wind blows through,
Where it came from is not quite known,
Where it's headed is anyone's guess
You can follow it,
But you'll never catch it
You can try to stop it,
But you'll never contain it.

To live without vision
It's to strive after the wind,
No clear direction to follow,
No purpose to define,
No goals to achieve.

But to chase after the wind seems comfortable,
It appears to be fun,
No bounds to hold you,
No set path to distract you,
No obstacles to delay you…

Striving after the wind,
It comes with a price
Never receiving
Never arriving
Never making it around the bend
Never fulfilled
Never grasping
Always striving

Acknowledgements

Shout out to my writing coach Jon Obermeyer. I've wanted to write a book for years. You've turned my dreams into a reality. Thank you.

Shout out to Scott Lacy. You've inspired and encouraged me to become a better writer. Thank you for believing in me.

Exposed, Nothing to Give, The Healing Road have sections that were inspired by paraphrases from the Bible.

The Sparrow - quote taken from the Hymn "His Eye is on the Sparrow" by Charles Gabriel and Civilla Martin

About Eric Hannan

Born in Ohio, Eric grew up in multiple states while his father served in the Navy. He now calls Raleigh, NC home, working as an Enterprise Agile Coach in the technology field.

When not at work, you'll find him traversing the country on his two tone, royal blue and black 111 cubic inch Indian Roadmaster or hanging out with his dog Chopper.

His favorite spot to ride is Deals Gap, a mountain pass on the North Carolina–Tennessee state line and home of highway 129, which bikers affectionately call the "Dragon's Tail." It boasts 318 turns in 11 miles, poetry in motion.

www.ingramcontent.com/pod-product-compliance
Lightning Source LLC
Chambersburg PA
CBHW061057050726
47592CB00004B/1718